bruschetta

crostini and other Italian snacks

MAXINE CLARK

bruschetta
crostini and other Italian snacks

PHOTOGRAPHY BY GUS FILGATE

RYLAND
PETERS
& SMALL
LONDON NEW YORK

First published in the USA in 2003
by Ryland Peters & Small, Inc.
519 Broadway, 5th Floor
New York, NY 10012
www.rylandpeters.com

10 9 8 7 6 5 4 3

     Library of Congress Cataloging-in-Publication Data
Clark, Maxine.
  Bruschetta, crostini, and other Italian snacks / Maxine Clark ;
photography by Gus Filgate.
     p. cm.
Includes index.
  ISBN 10: 1-84172-400-9
  ISBN 13: 978-1-84172-400-3
1. Cookery, Italian. 2. Appetizers. I. Title.
  TX723 .C5653 2003
  641.8'12'0945--dc21
                    2002151650

Printed in China

Designer Catherine Griffin
Commissioning Editor Elsa Petersen-Schepelern
Editor Sharon Ashman
Production Tamsin Curwood
Art Director Gabriella Le Grazie
Publishing Director Alison Starling

Food Stylist Maxine Clark
Assistant Food Stylist Becca Hetherston
Props Stylist Helen Trent

Notes
All spoon measurements are level
unless otherwise stated.

All eggs are medium, unless otherwise
specified. Uncooked or partly cooked
eggs should not be served to the very
young, the very old, the frail, or to
pregnant women.

contents

toast with taste ...

I first experienced bruschetta in an Italian friend's farmhouse in the beautiful Tuscan hills. We had just been out to collect sweet chestnuts and had done quite a bit of climbing to get to the trees. We were starving and it wasn't yet time for supper. So on our return, my friend decided to make us all *fettunta*—the Tuscan word for bruschetta rubbed with raw garlic and smeared with a ripe tomato. He toasted some huge, thick slices of Tuscan unsalted bread over some glowing embers on the hearth, cut a large juicy clove of garlic in half and rubbed it over the toasted bread, then sprinkled it with a local green, peppery olive oil. Finally, he spread a few roughly crushed tomatoes over the top. We devoured these bruschetta in our hands in front of the restoked fire—one of the best snacks I have ever eaten. And that is just what bruschetta are—satisfying snacks with peasant origins.

Crostini, on the other hand, are smaller, more refined snacks, usually baked in the oven or fried until crisp. These are elegantly served with pre-dinner drinks and are frequently offered as a matter of course in Italian bars. Crostoni, just larger crostini, are nice and crunchy, and vehicles for any combination of ingredients. In the northern regions of Italy, particularly the Veneto, crostini are made using fried or grilled polenta as the base. A very filling mouthful indeed, they have an interesting contrast of textures—crisp on the outside, soft inside.

Whatever their size or shape, all these snacks should be freshly made with the best ingredients. Bruschetta and crostini have sneaked their way into our modern lifestyles, appearing at smart dinner parties as starters and at cocktail parties as pre-dinner nibbles—far removed from their humble peasant origins, but none the worse for that. After all, we all love toast and to be truthful, that's what they are!

the basics

True bruschetta (and it is pronounced "brooskayta" not "brooshetta") is a large slice of country bread toasted on the barbecue or over a wood fire and then rubbed with garlic, sometimes topped with a crushed tomato, and anointed with olive oil. It is a popular snack found all over Italy, served in bars and at home. A true crostoni (large) or crostini (small) is brushed with olive oil and cooked in the oven or under the broiler, or fried in olive oil or butter.

bruschetta

4 thick slices country bread, preferably sourdough

2 garlic cloves, halved

extra virgin olive oil, for sprinkling

Serves 4

Grill, toast, or pan-grill the bread on both sides until lightly browned or toasted. Rub the top side of each slice with the cut garlic and sprinkle with olive oil. Keep in a warm oven before adding your chosen topping.

crostini

1 thin French baguette

extra virgin olive oil, for brushing

Serves 6

Preheat the oven to 375°F. Slice the bread into thin rounds, brush both sides with olive oil, and spread out on a baking sheet. Bake for about 10 minutes until crisp and golden. Let cool, then keep in an airtight container until ready to use. It is best to reheat them in the oven before adding the topping.

Crostoni are simply cut from a larger loaf and prepared in the same way as crostini.

polenta crostini

2 cups polenta flour

extra virgin olive oil, for brushing, or butter, for frying

Serves 6—8

Make the polenta by slowly sprinkling the flour into 1 quart of salted, boiling water. Cook over a low heat for 45 minutes, stirring occasionally. Turn out into a mound onto a wooden board. Let cool and set. Alternatively, use a quick-cooking version (cook according to the manufacturer's instructions), or the ready-made kind sold in a block. Slice the cooled and set polenta into the thickness you want, and cut or stamp out the required shape and size. Melt a little butter in a hot, nonstick skillet and cook until crisp, turning once. Alternatively, brush both sides with olive oil or melted butter and cook on a stove-top grill pan, turning once, if you prefer a grilled taste.

vegetables

A wonderful combination of fresh spring flavors and colors. Puréeing the peas gives a sweet, earthy base on which to sprinkle the combination of salty, nutty Pecorino (Parmesan would work very well here, too) and pears tossed in a few drops of balsamic vinegar for sharpness. A delicious start to a light dinner party.

pear, pecorino, and pea crostini

1 thin French baguette, sliced into thin rounds

extra virgin olive oil, for brushing and moistening

2 cups shelled fresh or frozen peas, about 8 oz.

freshly grated nutmeg

1 small ripe pear

a drop balsamic or sherry vinegar

1 cup fresh young Pecorino or Parmesan cheese, diced, about 4 oz.

sea salt and freshly ground black pepper

Serves 6

Preheat the oven to 375°F. To make the crostini, brush both sides of each slice of bread with olive oil, and spread out on a baking sheet. Bake for about 10 minutes until crisp and golden.

Meanwhile, blanch the peas in boiling water for 3 minutes if they are fresh, or 2 minutes if they are frozen. Drain them, refresh in cold water, and drain again. Purée the peas in a food processor or blender, moistening with a little olive oil. Season with salt, pepper, and freshly grated nutmeg. Core and finely chop the pear. Mix with a drop of balsamic or sherry vinegar, then add the cheese and mix well. Spread the crostini with a mound of pea purée and top with a spoonful of the pear and cheese mixture. Serve immediately.

slow-roasted tomatoes on bruschetta with salted ricotta or feta

These firm but juicy roasted tomatoes burst with the flavor of the sun. They take no time to prepare but a long time concentrating their flavors in the oven—they smell fantastic while cooking! Plum tomatoes have less moisture in them and work well. You can use other vine-ripened varieties—just make sure they have some taste!

Preheat the oven to 325°F. If using plum tomatoes, cut them in half lengthwise, if using round ones, cut them in half crosswise. Put them cut side up on a baking sheet. Mix the garlic and oregano with the olive oil, salt, and pepper. Spoon or brush this mixture over the cut tomatoes. Bake for about 2 hours, checking them occasionally. They should be slightly shrunk and still a brilliant red color. If they are too dark they will be bitter. Let cool.

To make the bruschetta, grill, toast, or pan-grill the bread on both sides until lightly browned or toasted. Cut the bruschetta slices to size so that 2 tomato halves will sit on top of each one. Rub the top side of each slice with the cut garlic, then sprinkle with olive oil.

Put 2 tomato halves on each bruschetta, top with the slivered cheese, and a basil leaf, if using. Serve at room temperature.

8 large ripe plum tomatoes

2 garlic cloves, finely chopped

1 tablespoon dried oregano

1/4 cup extra virgin olive oil

2 oz. salted ricotta or feta cheese, thinly sliced

sea salt and freshly ground black pepper

basil leaves, to serve (optional)

for the bruschetta:

4 thick slices country bread, preferably sourdough

2 garlic cloves, halved

extra virgin olive oil, for sprinkling

Serves 4

egg, mascarpone, and asparagus crostini

This is a creamy light topping, packed with the flavor of asparagus. For the best results, don't be tempted to make this with anything other than fresh asparagus. If you have some, you can sprinkle a little truffle oil over for a special occasion, as the flavors of eggs and truffle go very well together.

Preheat the oven to 375°F. To make the crostini, brush both sides of each slice of bread with olive oil, and spread out on a baking sheet. Bake for about 10 minutes until crisp and golden.

Meanwhile, beat the butter with the parsley and scallions and season with salt and pepper.

Cook the asparagus in boiling salted water for about 6 minutes until tender. Cut off and reserve the tips and slice the stems.

Boil the eggs for 6–8 minutes. Plunge into cold water for a couple of minutes, then shell and coarsely mash with a fork. Add the scallion mixture and mascarpone and stir until creamy. Fold in the sliced asparagus stems, then season with salt and pepper.

Spread the egg mixture thickly onto the crostini, top with the asparagus tips, and sprinkle with a couple drops of truffle oil, if using, or some extra virgin olive oil. Serve immediately.

1 thin French baguette, sliced into thin rounds
extra virgin olive oil, for brushing
$1/2$ cup unsalted butter, softened, about 4 oz.
$1/4$ cup chopped fresh parsley
4 scallions, finely chopped
12 spears fresh green asparagus, stems trimmed
6 large eggs
$1/4$—$1/3$ cup mascarpone cheese, softened
truffle oil, for sprinkling (optional)
sea salt and freshly ground black pepper

Serves 6

cherry tomato, bocconcini, and basil bruschetta

All the colors of the Italian flag are here—red, white, and green. This makes a great start to a rustic summer meal. Bocconcini (meaning "little bites") are tiny balls of mozzarella. They are the perfect size for bruschetta but, if you can't find them, use regular mozzarella instead and cut it into cubes.

Beat 3 tablespoons of the olive oil and the balsamic vinegar in a bowl. Season to taste with salt and pepper. Stir in the halved bocconcini or mozarella cubes, tomatoes, and torn basil leaves.

To make the bruschetta, grill, toast, or pan-grill the bread on both sides until lightly browned or toasted. Rub the top side of each slice with the cut garlic, then sprinkle with olive oil.

Cover each slice of bruschetta with arugula and spoon over the tomatoes and mozzarella. Sprinkle with the remaining olive oil and top with fresh basil leaves.

4 tablespoons extra virgin olive oil

1 teaspoon balsamic vinegar

12 bocconcini cheeses, halved, or 13 oz. regular mozzarella cheese, cubed

20 ripe cherry tomatoes or pomodorini (baby plum tomatoes), halved

a handful of torn fresh basil leaves, plus extra to serve

1 cup arugula

sea salt and freshly ground black pepper

for the bruschetta:

4 thick slices country bread, preferably sourdough

2 garlic cloves, halved

extra virgin olive oil, for sprinkling

Serves 4

white bean and black olive crostini

The combination of bland creamy beans and sharp, rich, salty tapenade makes a sublime mouthful, especially when spread on crisp crostini. You can use any type of canned bean for this, but the whiter they are the prettier they look. If you like, chop up some more black olives and sprinkle them on the bean purée or crumble some crisply cooked bacon over the top for extra crunch.

To make the tapenade, put the olives, garlic, anchovies, capers, and olive oil into a blender or food processor and blend until smooth. Scrape out into a jar, cover with a layer of olive oil, and set aside.

Preheat the oven to 375°F. To make the crostini, brush both sides of each slice of bread with olive oil, and spread out on a baking sheet. Bake for about 10 minutes until crisp and golden.

Meanwhile, make the bean purée. Heat the oil in a small skillet and add the garlic. Cook gently for 2 minutes until golden but don't let it turn brown. Stir in the rosemary and chile. Remove from the heat, add the beans and 3 tablespoons of water. Mash the beans coarsely with a fork and return to the heat until warmed through. Taste and season with salt and pepper.

Spread a layer of tapenade on the crostini followed by a spoonful of bean purée. Sprinkle with the chopped parsley and serve immediately.

for the tapenade:
6 oz Greek-style black olives, such as Kalamata, pitted, about 1½ cups

2 garlic cloves

3 canned anchovies, drained

2 teaspoons capers, drained

1 tablespoon olive oil

for the crostini:
1 thin French baguette, sliced into thin rounds

extra virgin olive oil, for brushing

for the white bean purée:
2 tablespoons olive oil

2 garlic cloves, finely chopped

1 teaspoon very finely chopped fresh rosemary

1 small red chile, seeded and finely chopped

1 lb. canned cannellini beans, rinsed and drained, about 1½ cups

sea salt and freshly ground black pepper

to serve:
chopped fresh parsley

Serves 6—8

The word *fettunta* comes from the Tuscan dialect and derives from Latin, meaning "anointed slice". It is a slice of bread grilled over hot coals, rubbed with garlic, and sprinkled with olive oil. To be authentic you should use only the finest Tuscan extra virgin olive oil. The ripe tomato is just crushed in your hand and smashed onto the bread, then eaten immediately. This is bruschetta at its simplest and best. This is a more civilized version, but you should try the real thing—it's great fun! Use only the best and freshest ingredients for this.

traditional peasant tomato and garlic bruschetta (*fettunta*)

4 large very ripe tomatoes

4 thick slices country bread, preferably sourdough

2 garlic cloves, halved

extra virgin olive oil, for sprinkling

sea salt and freshly ground black pepper

Serves 4

Coarsely chop the tomatoes and season with salt and pepper.

To make the bruschetta, grill, toast, or pan-grill the bread on both sides until lightly browned or toasted. Rub the top side of each slice with the cut garlic, then sprinkle with olive oil.

Spoon the tomatoes over the bruschetta and sprinkle with more olive oil. Eat immediately with your fingers!

olive oil and garlic bruschetta

This is pared-down simplicity and so easy to make. It beats the likes of doughballs and garlic bread hands down. The most important thing is not to overcook the garlic—it must on no account turn brown. This is great served instead of garlic bread with a selection of salads.

Slice the garlic lengthwise into paper-thin slices. Heat a small pan, pour in the olive oil, and stir in the garlic. Cook until the garlic starts to give off its aroma and is golden but not brown (or it will taste bitter). Remove from the heat, then mix in the chile flakes and parsley, if using. Cover to keep warm.

To make the bruschetta, grill, toast, or pan-grill the bread on both sides until lightly browned or toasted. Spoon or brush over the garlicky chile oil. Eat immediately with your fingers!

4 large garlic cloves

⅓ cup extra virgin olive oil

a good pinch chile flakes

¼ cup chopped fresh parsley (optional)

for the bruschetta:

4 thick slices country bread, preferably sourdough

extra virgin olive oil, for sprinkling

Serves 4

This is a joy to make when fresh artichokes are in season. After preparing the artichoke hearts, they are halved and fried in butter until tender. The pesto and pine nuts are perfect foils for the slightly bitter taste of the artichoke. If fresh ones are not available, you can use frozen or canned artichokes, or those preserved in oil. Whichever you use, always lightly fry them to bring out their full flavor.

artichoke, pesto, and pine nut bruschetta

To make the bruschetta, grill, toast, or pan-grill the bread on both sides until lightly browned or toasted. Rub the top side of each slice with the cut garlic, then sprinkle with olive oil. Keep in a warm oven.

Prepare the artichoke hearts (see note below) and cut them in half. Heat the oil and butter in a skillet, add the artichoke hearts, and fry gently until they are completely tender and beginning to brown. Splash in the balsamic vinegar, turn up the heat, and toss the artichoke hearts until the vinegar evaporates.

To make the pesto Genovese, put the garlic, pine nuts, Parmesan, basil leaves, olive oil, and seasoning in a blender or food processor and blend until smooth.

Spread the bruschetta with the pesto and divide the artichoke hearts between the slices. Top with the pine nuts and Parmesan shavings. Serve immediately.

Note: To prepare fresh artichoke hearts, first fill a bowl with water and squeeze in the juice of half a lemon. Use the other lemon half to rub the cut portions of the artichokes as you work. Trim the artichokes by snapping off the dark green outer leaves, starting at the base. Trim the stalk to about 2 inches and peel it. Cut about ⅛ inch off the tip of the artichoke heart, then place it in the lemony water until required.

4 thick slices country bread, preferably sourdough
2 garlic cloves, halved
extra virgin olive oil, for brushing

for the artichoke topping:
6 small, fresh artichokes, each about 3 inches long
2 tablespoons olive oil
2 tablespoons butter
1 tablespoon balsamic vinegar

for the pesto genovese:
2 garlic cloves
¼ cup pine nuts, about 2 oz.
¼ cup freshly grated Parmesan cheese
1½ cups fresh basil leaves
⅔ cup extra virgin olive oil
sea salt and freshly ground black pepper

to serve:
2 tablespoons pine nuts, toasted
shavings of Parmesan cheese

Serves 4

Preheat the oven to 475°F. Put the peppers into a large roasting pan and roast for 20–30 minutes, turning once, until they begin to brown. Remove from the oven and put into a plastic bag, seal tightly, and set aside for 10 minutes to steam off the skins.

Meanwhile, to make the bruschetta, grill or pan-grill the slices of bread on one side only until lightly browned or toasted. Rub the grilled sides with the cut garlic, then sprinkle with olive oil. Keep in a warm oven.

Remove the peppers from the bag and peel off the skins, then pull out the stalks—the seeds should come with them. Cut the peppers in half, scrape out any remaining seeds, and slice the flesh thickly.

To make the caper dressing, put the chopped capers into a bowl, then stir in the olive oil, vinegar, salt, and pepper.

Spread the pesto over the ungrilled side of the bruschetta and put 2 slices of cheese on each one. Cook under a preheated broiler for 1–2 minutes or until the cheese is beginning to melt and turn golden (watch that the bread doesn't catch fire and burn).

Remove from the heat and put a tangle of roasted peppers on top and spoon over the caper dressing. Serve immediately.

2 sweet red peppers

¼ cup Pesto Genovese (see page 25)

8 thick slices goat cheese with rind

for the bruschetta:

4 thick slices country bread, preferably sourdough

2 garlic cloves, halved

extra virgin olive oil, for sprinkling

for the caper dressing:

2 tablespoons salted capers, soaked in water for 10 minutes, then rinsed and chopped

3 tablespoons extra virgin olive oil

1 teaspoon balsamic vinegar

sea salt and freshly ground black pepper

Serves 4

goat cheese and sweet red peppers on bruschetta

Cooked goat cheese is a relative newcomer to Italian cuisine. When broiled, its sharp, creamy texture perfectly partners the smoky sweetness of roasted red peppers, especially when topped with salty, pungent capers and a little dressing.

garlic mushrooms with gremolata on bruschetta

A grown-up version of mushrooms on toast. Don't be tempted to use button or shiitake mushrooms: the first are too bland, the second too strong. If you have the good fortune to have some wild mushrooms, try a combination of porcini and girolles, or chanterelles. Make sure they don't become overcooked and soggy though. Top with a fried or poached egg for a substantial snack.

To make the bruschetta, preheat a stove-top grill pan, add the slices of bread, and cook on both sides until barred with brown. Brush with melted butter and keep in a warm oven.

To make the gremolata, put the garlic, lemon zest, parsley, and olives into a bowl. Stir well, cover, and chill.

Then, prepare the garlic mushrooms. Melt the butter or heat the olive oil in a skillet, add the shallots and garlic, and fry for 5 minutes until soft and golden. Add the mushrooms and toss well. Fry over high heat for 1 minute.

Add the wine and season with salt and pepper. Cook over high heat again until the wine evaporates. Stir in the parsley. Pile the mushrooms on the bruschetta and serve immediately, topped with a sprinkling of gremolata, if using.

4 thick slices country bread, preferably sourdough
melted butter, for brushing

for the black olive gremolata (optional):
1 small garlic clove, finely chopped
finely grated zest of 1 lemon
¼ cup chopped fresh flat-leaf parsley
16 Greek-style black olives, such as kalamata, pitted and chopped

for the garlic mushrooms:
⅓ cup butter or olive oil, about 3 oz.
3 shallots, finely chopped
2 garlic cloves, finely chopped
1¼ lb. large mushrooms, thickly sliced
⅓ cup dry white wine
3 tablespoons chopped fresh flat-leaf parsley
sea salt and freshly ground black pepper

Serves 4

Baba Ganoush is a Middle Eastern dip, usually served with a flatbread. It makes a perfect topping for crostini, and could almost be Sicilian with its mixture of eggplant and sesame seed flavors. Although sesame seed paste is unknown in Sicily, sesame seeds are commonly used in baking, especially to flavor breads.

baba ganoush crostini topped with crispy eggplant

Preheat a stove-top grill pan until very hot. Prick the eggplant all over with a sharp knife, then pan-grill, turning regularly, until blackened and completely soft. This will take about 20 minutes. Let cool slightly, then remove the charred skin. Coarsely chop the flesh, put it in a sieve, and let drain. Press to remove the bitter juices.

Put the eggplant flesh in a blender or food processor with the tahini, crushed garlic, and a pinch of hot paprika. Blend until well-mixed, then stir in the parsley or cilantro. Taste, then season with lemon juice, salt, and pepper.

 To make the crispy eggplant slices, heat the oil in a skillet, and add the thinly sliced eggplant. Cook until brown and crisp. Remove with a slotted spoon and drain on paper towels.

Preheat the oven to 375°F. To make the crostini, brush both sides of each slice of bread with olive oil, and spread out on a baking sheet. Bake for about 10 minutes until crisp and golden.

Put a slice of tomato on each crostini, season with salt, then spoon on a mound of baba ganoush, and top with a slice of crispy eggplant. Sprinkle with olive oil and hot paprika. Serve immediately.

1 eggplant, about 1 lb.

3 tablespoons tahini (sesame seed paste)

1 garlic clove, crushed

pinch hot paprika, plus extra for serving

2 tablespoons chopped fresh parsley or cilantro

juice of 1 lemon

3 large ripe tomatoes, very thinly sliced

extra virgin olive oil, for sprinkling

sea salt and freshly ground black pepper

for the crispy eggplant slices:

vegetable oil, for shallow frying

1 small eggplant, very thinly sliced

for the crostini:

1 thin French baguette, sliced into thin rounds

extra virgin olive oil, for brushing

Serves 6

fish

The contrast of strong flavors and interesting textures in this recipe transports you instantly to the shores of the Mediterranean. Use a combination of green and black olives if you prefer a sharper flavor. This mixture can be used as a stuffing for tomatoes, too.

tuna, black olive, pine nut, and caper
crostini

Preheat the oven to 375°F. To make the crostini, brush both sides of each slice of bread with olive oil, and spread out on a baking sheet. Bake for about 10 minutes until crisp and golden.

Put the olives, pine nuts, capers, garlic, parsley, tomatoes, and lemon rind in a bowl, and mix well. Add the tuna, break it up with a fork, and mix it thoroughly with the other ingredients. Moisten with a little olive oil, taste, and season with salt and pepper. Pile the mixture on top of the crostini. Serve immediately.

1 thin French baguette, thinly sliced diagonally

extra virgin olive oil, for brushing and moistening

1½ cups oven-baked or Greek-style black olives, pitted and chopped

2 tablespoons pine nuts, chopped

1 tablespoon chopped capers, drained

1 small garlic clove, finely chopped

1 tablespoon chopped fresh parsley

6 sun-dried tomatoes, soaked and chopped

1 tablespoon finely grated lemon rind

3¼ oz. canned tuna in oil, drained

sea salt and freshly ground black pepper

Serves 6

chile squid and deep-fried eggplant on bruschetta

The marinade tenderizes the squid and adds a kick of chile to its natural sweetness—the longer it is marinated, the more tender it will become. The eggplant can be fried in advance, then warmed up in the oven, leaving only the squid to be fried before serving. The arugula not only adds color, but a peppery sharpness to cut through the richness of the squid and eggplant. You can of course use frozen squid for this.

To make the marinade, put the chiles, garlic, lemon rind, lemon juice, sugar, and olive oil into a blender or food processor and blend until smooth. Stir the squid into the marinade, cover, and leave for 2 hours.

To make the bruschetta, grill, toast, or pan-grill the bread on both sides until lightly browned or toasted. Rub the top side of each slice with the cut garlic, then sprinkle with olive oil. Keep in a warm oven.

Preheat the oil in a wok or deep-fat fryer to 375°C or until a piece of stale bread turns golden in a few seconds when dropped in. Deep-fry the eggplant slices in batches until brown and crisp. Remove with a slotted spoon and drain on paper towels, then arrange in an even layer over the bruschetta. Keep in a warm oven.

Heat a heavy skillet until it is very hot and brush with oil. Remove the squid from the marinade and drain well, reserving the marinade. Sauté the squid for about 1 minute, tossing all the time until just caramelizing. Pour the marinade into the pan and boil rapidly for 30 seconds to reduce. Spoon the squid over the eggplant slices. Serve immediately with some arugula piled on top and lemon wedges, if using.

Note: To clean fresh squid, pull the head from the body. Remove the plastic quill from the inside of the squid tube, then rinse the tubes. Trim the tentacles from the head. Pop out the beak from the centre of the tentacles. Rinse, discarding the head and entrails.

1 lb. baby squid, cleaned and sliced (see note below)

vegetable oil, for deep-frying

1 small eggplant, very thinly sliced

sea salt and freshly ground black pepper

for the marinade:

2 small red chiles, seeded and chopped

2 garlic cloves

finely grated rind and juice of 1 lemon

1 tablespoon sugar

¼ cup olive oil

for the bruschetta:

4 thick slices country bread, preferably sourdough

2 garlic cloves, halved

extra virgin olive oil, for sprinkling

to serve:

1 cup arugula

lemon wedges (optional)

Serves 4

spicy garlic prawns with tomatoes and chickpeas on bruschetta

This is a very popular combination of ingredients in southern Italy. Sweet prawns and tomatoes contrast with earthy chickpeas, pungent garlic, and a hint of fiery chile. Great food for warm summer evenings in the garden.

Heat the oil in a large skillet and add the garlic, fry until just turning golden, then add the chile and wine. Turn up the heat and boil on high to reduce the wine to almost nothing. Add the tomatoes (if you are using canned tomatoes add some sugar to bring out their flavor) and cook for 1–2 minutes until they start to soften. Stir in the prawns and chickpeas and bring to a boil. Simmer for 2–3 minutes. Stir in the parsley, taste and season with salt and pepper. Set aside.

To make the bruschetta, grill, toast, or pan-grill the bread on both sides until lightly browned or toasted. Rub the top side of each slice with the cut garlic, then sprinkle with olive oil. Spoon over the prawn mixture and serve immediately.

2 tablespoons extra virgin olive oil

2 garlic cloves, finely chopped

1/2 teaspoon dried chile flakes

1/2 cup dry white wine

1/2 lb. ripe tomatoes, peeled and chopped, or canned tomatoes, chopped

1/2 teaspoon sugar (optional)

1/2 lb. raw, shelled prawns

1/4 cup canned chickpeas, rinsed and drained, about 2 oz.

2 tablespoons chopped fresh flat-leaf parsley

sea salt and freshly ground black pepper

for the bruschetta:

4 thick slices country bread, preferably sourdough

2 garlic cloves, halved

extra virgin olive oil, for sprinkling

Serves 4

Preheat the oven to 375°F. To make the crostini, brush both sides of each slice of bread with olive oil, and spread out on a baking sheet. Bake for about 10 minutes until crisp and golden. Let cool, then keep in an airtight container until ready to use. It is best to reheat them in the oven before adding the topping.

Cut the sole fillets diagonally across the grain into thin strips. Toss the strips in the seasoned flour and shake off the excess. Next, dip them into the beaten egg in batches, turning them until well coated. Give them a bit of a shake, then toss them in the breadcrumbs until evenly coated. Put them on a tray, making sure they don't touch, cover them with plastic wrap, and refrigerate.

To make the tartar sauce, beat the watercress into the mayonnaise, then fold in the tarragon, parsley, capers, and pickles. Taste and season well with salt and pepper.

Preheat the vegetable oil in a wok or deep-fat fryer to 375°C or until a piece of stale bread turns golden in a few seconds when dropped in. Fry a few sole sticks at a time until crisp and golden. Drain each batch well on paper towels, then sprinkle with salt. Keep in a warm oven with the door slightly ajar (they will get soggy if it is closed) while you cook the rest. Spread the crostini with a good dollop of tartar sauce, then top each one with 2 or 3 sole sticks. Serve with a few sprigs of watercress and some lemon wedges.

1 thin French baguette, sliced into thin rounds
extra virgin olive oil, for brushing
1/2 lb. thick sole fillets, skinned
2 tablespoons seasoned flour
1 egg, beaten
1/2—1 cup breadcrumbs, toasted
vegetable oil, for deep-frying
sea salt and freshly ground black pepper

for the watercress tartar sauce:
1/2 cup watercress leaves, blanched, squeezed dry and very finely chopped
1 1/4 cups mayonnaise
1 teaspoon finely chopped fresh tarragon
2 tablespoons chopped fresh parsley
1 tablespoon chopped capers, drained
2 tablespoons chopped pickles

to serve:
watercress sprigs
lemon wedges

Serves 6

goujons of sole with watercress tartar crostini

Crunchy sticks of freshly cooked sole sit on top of a delicious creamy, but sharp, tartar sauce tinged green with watercress. The difference between homemade and readymade tartar sauce is immense—so make your own for this recipe and you'll thank yourself in the end.

smoked salmon and lemon pepper cream crostini

This makes an elegant alternative to the usual smoked salmon canapés. The cream has a punchy pepper kick to it with cool lemon undertones. Tossing the salmon in the dill gives it a lovely fresh appearance.

Preheat the oven to 375°F. To make the crostini, brush both sides of each slice of bread with olive oil, and spread out on a baking sheet. Bake for about 10 minutes until crisp and golden. Let cool, then keep in an airtight container until ready to use. It is best to reheat them in the oven before adding the topping.

To make the lemon pepper cream, pound or grind the peppercorns as finely as possible. Beat the mascarpone with the ground pepper, add the milk and lemon rind, and beat again. Season with salt and lemon juice to taste. Chill until needed.

Toss the smoked salmon with the chopped dill. Spread the crostini with the lemon pepper cream and place a mound of smoked salmon on top. Squeeze over a little more lemon juice and serve immediately.

½ lb. thinly sliced smoked salmon
2 tablespoons chopped fresh dill
sea salt

for the crostini:
1 thin French baguette, thinly sliced diagonally
extra virgin olive oil, for brushing

for the lemon pepper cream:
2 teaspoons black peppercorns
⅓ cup mascarpone cheese
⅓ cup milk
finely grated rind and juice of 1 lemon

Serves 6

This is the Italian equivalent of Mexican tacos but turned upside down. The crisply fried polenta bases remain soft in the middle and are topped with chunky guacamole and smoky pan-grilled strips of chicken. The contrast of flavors and textures is amazing.

pan-grilled chicken and guacamole
on crisp polenta crostini

¼ lb. skinless, boneless chicken breasts

2 tablespoons lemon juice

1 garlic clove, crushed

2 tablespoons olive oil

1 recipe Polenta Crostini (see page 9)

butter, for frying, or olive oil or melted butter, for brushing

for the guacamole:

2 ripe avocados

6 scallions, chopped

1 medium tomato, skinned, seeded and chopped

2 tablespoons chopped fresh cilantro

lemon juice

sea salt and freshly ground black pepper

to serve:

3 cherry tomatoes, halved

cilantro

Serves 6

Cut the chicken into finger-thin strips and mix with the lemon juice, garlic, and olive oil. Leave to marinate while you make the guacamole.

Halve the avocados, remove the stones and peel off the skin. Place the flesh in a bowl and mash to a coarse texture with a fork. Mix in the scallions, chopped tomato, and cilantro. Season to taste with lemon juice, salt and pepper. Don't make this too far in advance as the mixture discolors quickly.

To cook the polenta crostini, melt a little butter in a hot, nonstick skillet and cook until crisp, turning once. Alternatively, brush both sides with olive oil or melted butter and pan-grill, turning once, for a grilled taste.

To cook the chicken, heat a stove-top grill pan until smoking. Add the chicken strips and pan-grill on one side only for 2—3 minutes, without moving, until cooked.

Spread the crostini with some guacamole, then top with some pan-grilled chicken strips. Place half a cherry tomato and some cilantro on each one. Serve immediately.

meat and poultry

grilled fig and prosciutto
bruschetta **with arugula**

This combination of caramelized figs and crisply barbecued prosciutto is irresistible. The figs are best cooked on a barbecue, but you can use a stove-top grill pan or a broiler—just get the right amount of browning on the figs.

To make the bruschetta, grill, toast, or pan-grill the bread on both sides until lightly browned or toasted. Rub the top side of each slice with the cut garlic, then sprinkle with olive oil. Keep in a warm oven.

Take the figs and stand them upright. Using a small, sharp knife, make two cuts across each fig not quite quartering it, but keeping it intact at the base. Ease the figs open and brush with balsamic vinegar and olive oil. Put the figs cut side down on a preheated barbecue or stove-top grill pan and cook for 3—4 minutes until hot and slightly browned—don't move them during cooking. Alternatively, place the figs cut side up under a really hot broiler until browning and heated through.

While the figs are cooking, place half the slices of prosciutto on the barbecue or stove-top grill pan, or under the broiler, and cook until frazzled. Remove and keep warm while cooking the remaining slices. Place two figs, three pieces of prosciutto, and some arugula on each slice of bruschetta. Cover with Parmesan shavings and sprinkle with olive oil. Serve immediately.

4 thick slices country bread, preferably sourdough

2 garlic cloves, halved

extra virgin olive oil, for sprinkling, plus extra for brushing

8 ripe fresh figs

2 tablespoons balsamic vinegar

12 slices prosciutto

1 cup arugula

sea salt and freshly ground black pepper

shavings of Parmesan cheese, to serve

Serves 4

chorizo with crunchy saffron potatoes
on bruschetta

This pretty-colored substantial snack has its origins in Spain. The secret ingredient is a mild smoked paprika called *pimentón*, which gives the potatoes an interesting depth of flavor. If you can't get hold of it, use sweet paprika instead.

Peel the potatoes and cut into 1 inch cubes. Cook in boiling salted water for 5–7 minutes until they are almost cooked, but still slightly firm in the middle.

While the potatoes are cooking, make the bruschetta. Grill, toast, or pan-grill the bread on both sides until lightly browned or toasted. Rub the top side of each slice with the cut garlic, then sprinkle with olive oil. Keep in a warm oven.

Drain the potatoes well. Heat the sunflower oil in a large skillet, add the potatoes and fry them over medium heat for about 5 minutes, turning from time to time, until a light golden brown. Sprinkle the saffron water over the potatoes and continue to cook for 3–4 minutes. Next, add the ground cumin and pimentón and cook for a further 5 minutes, tossing and turning the potatoes until they build up a nice spicy crust. Add the chorizo and cook for another 5 minutes until it is heated through.

Season well with salt and pepper, then spoon the mixture over the bruschetta. Sprinkle with fresh cilantro and serve immediately.

³/₄ lb. potatoes

4 thick slices country bread, preferably sourdough

2 garlic cloves, halved

extra virgin olive oil, for sprinkling

2—3 tablespoons sunflower oil

large pinch saffron threads soaked in 3 tablespoons hot water for 15 minutes

¹/₂ teaspoon ground cumin

¹/₂ teaspoon pimentón (smoked paprika)

6 oz. chorizo, sliced or cubed

sea salt and freshly ground black pepper

chopped fresh cilantro, to serve

Serves 4

These are delicious mouthfuls of melting mozzarella swathed in Parma ham. They taste good served cold with the addition of a thin slice of ripe melon on top, but heating them up transforms them.

prosciutto-wrapped bocconcini crostini

Preheat the oven to 375°F. To make the crostini, brush both sides of each slice of bread with olive oil, and spread out on a baking sheet. Bake for about 10 minutes until crisp and golden. Let cool, then keep in an airtight container until ready to use. It is best to reheat them in the oven before adding the topping.

Put a sage leaf on top of each bocconcini or mozzarella cube and season with salt and pepper. Cut each slice of ham into three equal pieces and wrap up a piece of cheese in each one.

Mix the mustard and balsamic vinegar together and spread on the crostini. Put two wrapped mozzarellas on top of each crostini and place on a baking sheet. Bake in the oven for 3–5 minutes or until the cheese just melts. Serve immediately, sprinkled with more sage leaves.

1 thin French baguette, sliced into thin rounds

extra virgin olive oil, for brushing

24 fresh sage leaves, plus extra to serve

24 bocconcini cheeses or 26 oz. mozzarella cheese, cubed

8 slices prosciutto or Parma ham

3 tablespoons wholegrain mustard

1 teaspoon balsamic vinegar

sea salt and freshly ground black pepper

Serves 6

To make the salsa verde, pound the salt and garlic with a mortar and pestle until creamy. Stir in the anchovies, parsley, mint, basil, capers, olive oil, lemon juice, and pepper. Transfer to a jar and pour a layer of olive oil on top to exclude the air. This will keep for up to a week in the refrigerator.

To make the bruschetta, grill, toast, or pan-grill the bread on both sides until lightly browned or toasted. Rub the top side of each slice with the cut garlic, then sprinkle with olive oil. Keep in a warm oven.

Wrap the beef tightly in plastic wrap and put into the freezer for 20 minutes or until just beginning to freeze. Using a very sharp, thin-bladed knife, slice the beef into paper-thin slices (the part-freezing will make this easier). If you find this difficult, cut it as thinly as you can, then gently pound it out between two sheets of plastic wrap, without breaking through the flesh. This should be done at the last minute, or the meat will discolor.

Brush the bruschetta with a little salsa verde, then drape the sliced beef over the top. Spoon on some more salsa verde and top with a mound of wild arugula, and a few Parmesan shavings. Season with salt and pepper, and serve immediately.

4 thick slices of country bread, preferably sourdough

2 garlic cloves, halved

extra virgin olive oil, for sprinkling

1/2 lb. best fillet of beef, perfectly trimmed

1 cup wild arugula

sea salt and freshly ground black pepper

shavings of Parmesan cheese, to serve

for the salsa verde:

1 teaspoon sea salt

2 garlic cloves, finely chopped

4 anchovy fillets in oil, rinsed

3 tablespoons chopped fresh parsley

3 tablespoons chopped fresh mint

3 tablespoons chopped fresh basil

2 tablespoons salted capers, rinsed and chopped

2/3 cup cold-pressed extra virgin olive oil, plus extra for sealing

2 tablespoons lemon juice

freshly ground black pepper

Serves 4

carpaccio of beef with salsa verde on bruschetta

This colorful dish relies on using the best beef fillet you can buy, thinly sliced and served with the classic Italian caper and herb sauce. Carpaccio of beef was created by the original owner of Harry's Bar in Venice. The colors of the dish reminded him of the paintings of the Venetian Renaissance artist, Carpaccio, and the name stuck. This is a lighter dressing than the original version, which included mustard and egg yolks.

italian sausage with radicchio and taleggio
on crisp polenta crostoni

There is nothing more delicious on a cool autumnal evening than a golden polenta crostoni fried or grilled until crisp, topped with succulent Italian pork sausage, covered with melting Taleggio cheese and sweetly soft radicchio. You could be in front of a roaring fire in the Tuscan hills.

Preheat a skillet, broiler, or stove-top grill pan. Cut the polenta into four thick slices, slightly smaller than the size of your hand (these are now crostoni). To cook the polenta crostoni, melt a little butter in a hot, nonstick skillet, and cook until crisp, turning once. Alternatively, brush both sides of the crostoni with olive oil or melted butter and broil or pan-grill on both sides.

Quarter the radicchio and remove the bitter white core. Put the leaves cut side up on a preheated stove-top grill pan. Brush with olive oil and season with salt and pepper. Add the sausages to the pan and pan-grill for about 10 minutes until the sausages are cooked and the radicchio has softened and is a little browned.

Meanwhile, remove the rind from the cheese and slice thickly. Slice the cooked sausages thickly, too. Put the cooked polenta slices on a lined broiler pan and cover with the sausage slices. Top each crostoni with a couple sage leaves and then a piece of radicchio, then cover each one with a layer of sliced cheese. Place under a hot broiler and broil until the cheese is melted and bubbling. Serve immediately.

1 recipe Polenta Crostini (see page 9)

butter, for frying, or olive oil or melted butter, for brushing

1 small radicchio

2 tablespoons olive oil, for brushing

4 fat Italian pork sausages (or any other high-meat content butcher's sausage)

4—5 oz. Taleggio or Fontina cheese (or other nutty quick-melting cheese)

8 fresh sage leaves

sea salt and freshly ground black pepper

Serves 4

other Italian snacks

parmesan crisps

You'll never make enough of these thin, crunchy savory crisps—the secret is not to cook them for too long. They are sometimes made in a skillet, but it is much easier to bake them in quantity in the oven. They keep well in an airtight container. I prefer to use Grana Padano for this—it is cheaper than Parmesan and works just as well.

Preheat the oven to 400°F. Line a baking sheet with nonstick baking parchment. Spoon small mounds of grated cheese onto the paper at regular intervals. Flatten with the back of the spoon. Sprinkle a few fennel seeds or some chopped red chile on top, if you like.

Bake for 3–6 minutes until golden. Remove from the oven and leave for a couple minutes to set. You can curl them over a wooden spoon handle or rolling pin at this stage to give a more interesting shape, if you like. Carefully lift them off the paper. Let cool completely on a baking rack. These crisps will keep for up to 4 days if stored in an airtight container.

1 cup freshly grated Grana Padano or Parmesan cheese, about 4 oz.

a few fennel seeds (optional)

1 red chile, seeded and finely chopped (optional)

Serves 4

A wonderful explosion of the flavors of sage and anchovy through crisp batter. These must be served virtually straight out of the pan. I like to use a packet of Japanese tempura batter for this—it is so light and crisp.

deep-fried sage leaves

Wash and dry the sage leaves. Mash the capers with the anchovy paste and spread onto the darker green sides of 12 of the leaves. Press another leaf on top of the filling to form a sandwich.

If you're not using Japanese tempura batter, then make your own. Lightly beat the egg and the ice water together. Add the flour and beat again, leaving the mixture a bit lumpy. Do not allow to stand.

Heat the oil in a deep pan or wok until a piece of stale bread turns golden in a few seconds when dropped in. Holding the leaves by the stem, dip them into the batter, and lightly shake off the excess. Place into the hot oil, a few at a time, and fry until crisp and barely golden. This will only take a few seconds. Drain on paper towels and serve immediately.

24 large sage leaves

1 teaspoon salted capers, rinsed

1 tablespoon anchovy paste

vegetable oil, for deep-frying

for the batter:

1 egg

$2/3$ cup ice water

1 cup all-purpose flour

Makes 12

grissini

These long, thin crisp breadsticks originate from Turin in northern Italy. Once you have made your own, you will never want the readymade ones in packages again.

Preheat the oven to 400°F. Roll the dough out thinly on a well-floured surface to form a rectangle. Cut into ¼ inch strips along the long side of the rectangle. Lightly roll these strips with your fingers and taper the ends. Put them on a baking sheet, spacing well apart.

Brush the dough lightly with water and sprinkle with the flavouring of your choice. Bake for 5–8 minutes until crisp and brown. Let cool completely. Twist salami or prosciutto around the sticks, to serve, if using.

1 recipe Basic Pizza Dough (see below)

salami or prosciutto slices, to serve

flavorings:

sea salt

sesame seeds

poppy seeds

cracked black pepper

Makes about 40

basic pizza dough

In a medium bowl, cream the fresh yeast with the sugar and beat in 1 cup warm water. Leave for 10 minutes until frothy. For other yeasts, follow the manufacturer's instructions. Sift the flour into a large bowl and make a well in the center. Pour in the yeast mixture, olive oil, and salt. Mix together with a round-bladed knife, then use your hands to bring the dough together.

Turn out onto a floured surface, wash your hands, and knead for 10 minutes until smooth and elastic. The dough should be quite soft, but if too soft to handle, add more flour. Place in a clean oiled bowl, cover with a damp dishcloth and leave to rise until doubled in size—about 1 hour. Punch down and use as required.

½ oz. fresh yeast, ¼ oz. (1 envelope) active dry yeast or ¼ oz. (1 envelope) rapid-rise yeast

pinch sugar

1½ cups Italian 00 flour or all-purpose flour, plus extra for dusting

1 tablespoon olive oil

½ teaspoon sea salt

Makes 1 x 10—12-inch thin-crust pizza base

These are a great example of Sicilian street food—little fritters made out of ground chickpeas. So popular throughout the Mediterranean, every country has a form of snack made with these versatile legumes. The fritters are crisp on the outside and soft in the middle. To taste their best they must be served hot and sprinkled with lots of sea salt.

sicilian chickpea and rosemary fritters (*panelle*)

Lightly oil a cold surface such as a marble slab or the back of a large baking sheet. Have a spatula at the ready! Sift the chickpea flour into a saucepan. Beat in the water slowly, making sure there are no lumps. Stir in the rosemary, and salt and pepper to taste. Bring to a boil, beating all the time, until the mixture really thickens and leaves the side of the pan (like choux pastry). Don't worry if you get lumps at this stage, they will disappear when you fry the panelle.

Now you need to work really quickly. Tip the mixture onto the oiled surface and spread it out as thinly and evenly as you can—aim to make it about ⅙-inch thick. Let cool and set.

When set, cut into small triangles or squares. To prevent them drying out, place them between layers of plastic wrap until ready to cook. Heat some oil in a wok or deepfat fryer. The oil is ready when a piece of mixture will sizzle instantly when dropped in. Deep-fry a few panelle at a time, turning when golden brown. Drain on paper towels and sprinkle with salt. Serve hot.

2⅓ cups chickpea flour*, about 11 oz.

3 cups water

1—2 tablespoons chopped fresh rosemary

vegetable oil, for deep-frying

sea salt and freshly ground black pepper

Makes about 40

* Chickpea flour is known as gram flour in Indian shops.

mozzarella in carozza

A classic Italian restaurant favorite, but this more rustic version is so easy to make at home. The mozzarella melts inside the crisp bread coat, revealing a surprise of sun-dried tomatoes and anchovies inside.

Arrange the mozzarella slices over 4 of the slices of bread. Sprinkle the sun-dried tomatoes, anchovy fillets, and oregano over the mozzarella. Season well with salt and pepper, then put the remaining bread slices on top. Press down well.

Pour the beaten eggs into a large dish and dip the sandwiches in the egg, turning once to coat both sides. Leave them to soak up the egg for 30 minutes.

Heat the oil in a deep skillet until a crumb dropped in sizzles instantly. Fry each sandwich for 1–2 minutes on each side until crisp and golden brown. Drain on paper towels and serve piping hot.

18 oz. mozzarella cheese, thickly sliced

8 thin oval slices country bread

8 sun-dried tomatoes, soaked until soft and cut into strips

8 anchovy fillets in oil, drained

2 teaspoons dried oregano

3 eggs, beaten

vegetable oil, for shallow frying

sea salt and freshly ground black pepper

Serves 4

index

Conversion Chart

Weights and measures have been rounded up or down slightly to make measuring easier.

volumes:

American	metric	imperial
1 teaspoon	5 ml	
1 tablespoon	15 ml	
¼ cup	60 ml	2 fl.oz.
⅓ cup	75 ml	2½ fl.oz.
½ cup	125 ml	4 fl.oz.
⅔ cup	150 ml	5 fl.oz. (¼ pint)
¾ cup	175 ml	6 fl.oz.
1 cup	250 ml	8 fl.oz.

weights:

imperial	metric
1 oz.	25 g
2 oz.	50 g
3 oz.	75 g
4 oz.	125 g
5 oz.	150 g
6 oz.	175 g
7 oz.	200 g
8 oz.	250 g
9 oz.	275 g
10 oz.	300 g
11 oz.	325 g
12 oz.	375 g
13 oz.	400 g
14 oz.	425 g
15 oz.	475 g
1 lb.	500 g
2 lb.	1 kg

measurements:

inches	cm
¼ inch	5 mm
½ inch	1 cm
¾ inch	1.5 cm
1 inch	2.5 cm
2 inches	5 cm
3 inches	7 cm
4 inches	10 cm
5 inches	12 cm
6 inches	15 cm
7 inches	18 cm
8 inches	20 cm
9 inches	23 cm
10 inches	25 cm
11 inches	28 cm
12 inches	30 cm

oven temperatures:

225°F	110°C	Gas ¼
250°F	120°C	Gas ½
275°F	140°C	Gas 1
300°F	150°C	Gas 2
325°F	160°C	Gas 3
350°F	180°C	Gas 4
375°F	190°C	Gas 5
400°F	200°C	Gas 6
425°F	220°C	Gas 7
450°F	230°C	Gas 8
475°F	240°C	Gas 9